CW00419318

Contents

Introduction

We are the navigation authority responsible for the Rivers Wye and Lugg. It's our job to look after the environment and the navigation for these rivers.

The Wye Navigation Advisory Committee (WNAC) assists us in developing sustainable recreation and navigation on the river. The group was set up in 2003 and operates under an independent chairperson. Members represent a wide range of user interests, including pleasure craft operators, canoeists, rowers, landowners, local authorities and those with angling wildlife and conservation interests.

The River Wye at Symonds Yat

The River Wye

The Wye Valley is an important area for tourism, attracting many thousands of visitors each year. The river is a unique resource for sport and recreation. It is important for many activities as well as canoeing, including game fishing (mainly for salmon), coarse fishing, rafting, rowing, walking, bird watching and picnicking.

The River Wye is about 250km long and one of the longest rivers in Britain. It is mostly unaltered with no large man-made structures such as weirs on the main stem of the river or on most of the tributaries. The Wye rises in the Cambrian Mountains on Plynlimon before meeting the Severn Estuary at the fortress town of Chepstow. Close to its source, the river is characterised by still, shallow, gravelly stretches mixed with rocky cascades. The river is narrow and fast flowing through the high hills and rugged terrain towards Hay-on-Wye. From Hay to Whitney, the Wye flows between the Black Mountains and the Radnorshire Hills. Here the river is generally shallow, with minor rapids and several long pools. From Whitney to Hereford, the character of the river changes as it meanders through a broad floodplain. Below Bredwardine, the channel narrows before entering a wide valley with high banks upstream of Ross-on-Wye. From here, the river enters perhaps the most dramatic section, with spectacular views and deep wooded gorges down to Chepstow where it enters the Severn Estuary.

Walking at Ross-on-Wye

Conservation of wildlife

The River Wye is a Site of Special Scientific Interest (SSSI) and Special Area of Conservation (SAC) under the European Habitats Directive. Also the lower river from Mordiford to Chepstow is an Area of Outstanding Natural Beauty (AONB) and is regarded as one of the finest lowland landscapes in Britain. Some of the plants and animals found along the river are of international importance. Below are just some of the species that you might see along your journey.

Otter

Otters now range all over the River Wye catchment and its main tributaries, including the River Lugg. They can grow to the size of a medium-sized dog, and are largely nocturnal mammals. A lot of patience and luck is required to spot one. However, you can see signs of otters as you canoe down the Wye and the Lugg: footprints at the edge of muddy banks and droppings ('spraints') on rocks are the obvious signs to look out for. It is an offence under the Wildlife and Countryside Act 1981 to kill, injure or take an otter from the wild without a licence; to damage or obstruct an otter's den (holt) or disturb an otter in its resting place. You should take care not to disturb any dense vegetation, tree roots or rocky cavities that might harbour an otter, especially during the daytime and when looking for a suitable entry or exit point to the river.

Otter

Water-crowfoot

White clawed crayfish

These are the UK's only native freshwater crayfish and the River Wye system is the best site known in Wales for them. Crayfish are naturally found amongst stones in the river bed and bank, and amongst tree roots and in other cavities such as stone walls. They favour clean water habitats and are therefore sensitive to pollution.

There are some serious threats to the survival of this native species by the introduction of the North American signal crayfish. This non-native crayfish competes for food and habitat, and carries the crayfish plague. This fungal plague is also carried in water and on equipment such as wetsuits, canoes and fishing equipment that have been in contact with infected water or crayfish. It's important that you make sure all

equipment is dried thoroughly before you use it again in another river to kill the infection.

It is an offence under the *Wildlife and Countryside Act* to take or sell native freshwater crayfish from the wild.

Water-crowfoot

There are several different species of this aquatic plant found along the upper and lower reaches of the river. In the summer, the plant can form extensive mats, and produces flowers that add to the beauty and character of the river.

Water-crowfoot forms part of a habitat that helps give the River Wye its SAC Status. It is illegal to remove it without consent from Natural England or the Countryside Council for Wales. If you are experiencing problems navigating the river as a result of extensive

growth of this plant, please contact one of the Environment Agency's Biodiversity Officers on **029 2024 5256** for advice; they will be happy to help.

Salmon

The Wye Atlantic salmon population is of considerable importance in UK terms and, historically, the river is the most productive in Wales for this fish. Modification of the river has been kept to a minimum, thereby protecting important spawning habitat.

Salmon require a good flow of clean water over an exposed gravel bed for spawning. Migration up the river generally occurs between October and January, with spawning usually occurring in late winter. Eggs are buried in the gravel in nests known as "redds", with fry emerging in May.

During these months, you should take care not to disturb or damage areas of gravel bed that may appear to have been recently disturbed, as these are likely to be redds.

Other species that are found in the River Wye, and which also give the river its SAC status, include: sea lamprey, brook lamprey, river lamprey, twaite shad and bullhead.

If you require any further information on any of the above species, you can contact your local Biodiversity Officer on **029 2024 5256** or Fisheries Officer on **029 2024 5289**. Natural England and the Countryside Council for Wales can also provide information on the SSSI and SAC designation and designated features.

Navigation and recreational advice

Navigation rights and access

The River Wye has been used for navigation for many centuries. In the past the Wye was an important commercial waterway but, the infrastructure that supports this, such as locks and weirs, has long since been removed. Today, boating on the river is mostly canoeing and rowing, but with some passenger sightseeing boats operating around Symonds Yat.

A public right of navigation extends from Bigsweir Bridge upstream to Hay Town Bridge on the main River Wye, and on the River Lugg between its confluence with the Wye and Presteigne Town Bridge. The combined length of the non-tidal navigation on the Rivers Wye and Lugg (the part for which we are the navigation authority) is approximately 185 kilometres. The Gloucester Harbour Trustees are the navigation authority for the tidal section of the River Wye downstream of Bigsweir Bridge.

The public right of navigation below Hay does not give a right of access to the riverbank and other than at accepted public sites, you must get permission from the landowner before launching and landing canoes. Permission is also needed to camp or picnic on the banks or neighbouring fields.

Canoes at Symonds Yat

The Rivers Wye and Lugg navigation

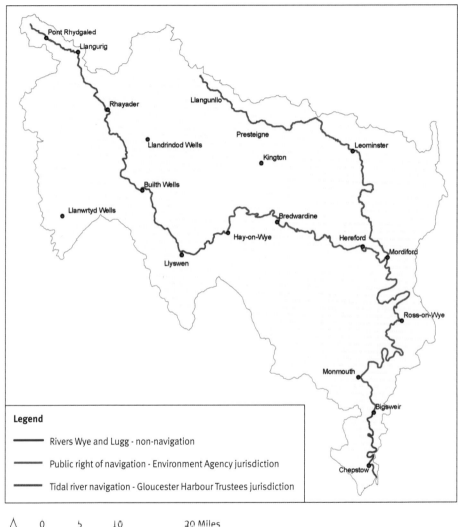

Legend

Rivers Wye and Lugg - non-navigation

Public right of navigation - Environment Agency jurisdiction

Tidal river navigation - Gloucester Harbour Trustees jurisdiction

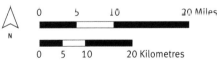

0   5   10   20 Miles

0   5   10   20 Kilometres

© Crown Copyright. All rights reserved. Environment Agency 100026380, (2007)

Canoeing on the River Wye

On the main river above Hay-on-Wye, the boating activity is almost exclusively canoeing. You can canoe continuously for 133km (the length of the public right to navigate from Hay Town Bridge to Bigsweir) which makes the Wye a great river for long distance touring. For this reason it is popular with Duke of Edinburgh expeditions as well as many canoe enthusiasts.

White water canoeing is enjoyed on parts of the upper river catchment. The rapids at Symonds Yat are a nationally important canoeing site owned by the British Canoe Union (BCU). There are a number of commercial canoe hire firms and adventure holiday companies based on the Wye, offering canoe and kayak trips.

Upper Wye Canoe Access Agreement

Upstream of Hay Bridge, the river can provide some good canoeing water but there is no established public right of navigation. An agreement exists that facilitates shared access between the anglers and paddlers.

Canoeing these upper reaches is considered at its best during the high flows of autumn and winter, while fishing takes place during drier months, giving the opportunity for an amicable sharing of the river. The agreed dates for canoe access are 18 October to 15 March inclusive for the upper Wye. However, under the agreement, canoeing is possible outside these dates when river levels are above the red markers on two gauges, which you can check on the Wye and Usk Foundation website - **www.wyeuskfoundation.org/ conditions/index.php.** This allows for paddling every day when water conditions are best for adventurous canoeing. The agreement secured access and egress points and provided signage and maps.

Representatives from local Outdoor Centres, riparian owners, Countryside Council for Wales, Environment Agency, and the British Outdoor Professionals Association, led by the

Kayaking at Symonds Yat

Wye and Usk Foundation, were responsible for delivering the arrangements.

The upper Wye is not recommended for beginners or canoeists that do not have considerable experience of white water.

To avoid problems, it is essential that everyone who uses the river acts responsibly and follows advice in the Wye code of conduct.

Remember - there are many users of the Wye. Please respect their wishes and needs!

River gradings

The following classifications are used by the Welsh Canoeing Association (WCA) on the canoewales.com website to describe the level of difficulty. The grading of rivers is very difficult, with differing opinions amongst paddlers, and as a result any classification is very subjective and dependant on conditions.

Grade I – Easy: moving water with the odd disturbances in the shape of small, regular waves and slight meanders.

Grade II – Moderate: the water is faster and rapids are more frequent; rocks, waves and small stoppers are found but always with an obvious channel.

Grade III – Harder: the pace quickens with fairly big waves and stoppers which are quite capable of holding a boat firmly. Rapids are much more continuous and, although the route is fairly obvious, it is necessary to be able to manoeuvre the kayak well.

Grade IV – Difficult: long stretches of heavy rapids and falls with irregular waves and often powerful holding stoppers. The route is not obvious from the water, and bank inspection is usually necessary. A mistake or swim could be serious.

Grade V – Extremely difficult: longer rapids, large drops with very big waves, dangerous stoppers and rocks to negotiate. This is a challenge to any canoeist. Although never absent in the lower grades, in grade V, substantial danger is always a possibility. Continual inspection and/or protection are often necessary.

Grade VI – Limit of navigation: a line down exists – just. Luck may often play a part. There is always a real risk to life. Very favourable water conditions and protection may make rapids of this grade feasible. Very skilful paddling and the ability to pick the ideal days are also involved. Most of the time, they are too dangerous to canoe.

Gradings for the River Wye

A description of the river gradings for the various stretches of rivers as described in the canoewales.com website is summarised below.

Stretch	Length	Grade	Notable Features
Pont Rhydygaled to Llangurig	8 km	II	
Llangurig to Rhayader	17 km	III(IV)	
Rhayader Falls		III or IV (IV in high water)	Rapids/falls
Rhayader to Builth Wells	26 km	II - III	Rapids
Builth Wells to Llyswen	20 km	II – III (IV)	Rapids, no portages
Llyswen to Hay-on-Wye	16 km	I	
Hay-on-Wye to Brewardine	25 km	I	
Brewardine to Hereford	27 km	I - II	
Hereford to Ross-on-Wye	49 km	I	
Ross-on-Wye to Monmouth	39 km	I - II	Symonds Yat Rapids
Monmouth to Chepstow	33 km	I - II	

Gradings for the River Wye

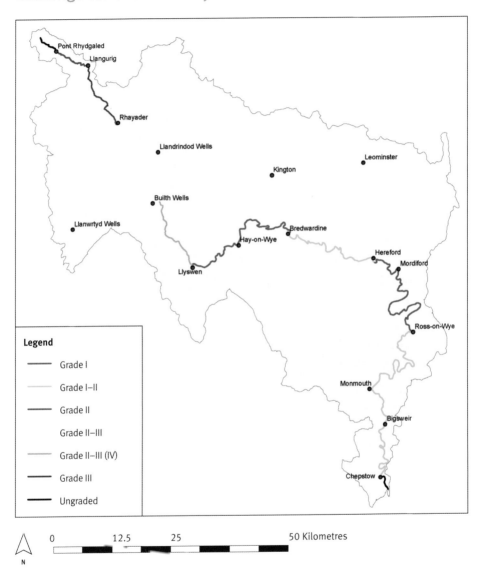

Legend

— Grade I

— Grade I–II

— Grade II

Grade II–III

— Grade II–III (IV)

— Grade III

— Ungraded

0   12.5   25   50 Kilometres

N

© Crown Copyright. All rights reserved. Environment Agency 100026380, (2007)

BCU and WCA contacts

WCA Regional Officer:
Pam Bell, Rose Cottage,
Llanelli Hill, Upper Cwm Nantgam,
Abergavenny, NP7 0RF
Tel: 01873 831 825

BCU Local River Advisor:
(Hay-on-Wye to Symonds Yat):
Stephen Phillips, 1 Knights Way,
Newent, Gloucester GL18 1QJ
Tel: 01531 822 614
steve@sandmphillips.fsnet.co.uk

BCU Local Access Officer:
(downstream of Monmouth)
Graham Symonds, 7 White Hill Close,
Monmouth, NP5 4FG
Tel: 01600 713 461

Canoe hire and instruction

Several companies in the Wye Valley
offer canoes for hire and instruction,
and will guide groups of canoelsts.
For details contact local Tourist
Information Centres.

Kayaking at Monmouth

Good practice guidelines

Our aim is to see the river used respectfully by all parties and in a way that is sensitive to the many environmental designations. In order to achieve harmony we have produced a code of conduct. Below is some general information included in the code.

Salmon and trout lay their eggs in gravel between October and April. Trampling and launching canoes on gravels used by salmon may damage their eggs and young fry. This is of particular concern upstream of Glasbury, and when the water level is low.

Game stocks are now a scarce resource so please do not canoe if the risk of disturbance is high. While coarse fish stocks are not in danger it is worth remembering that they spawn between April and July, and so unnecessary disturbance of gravels should be avoided at these times.

In May and June, two rare and protected species of migratory fish, Allis and Twaite shad, are present and breeding in fast flowing gravelly areas of the river. It is an offence to damage or destroy these spawning areas, so canoeists must avoid trampling or dragging canoes across these parts of the river during these months.

The Wye is also an important habitat for a variety of birds and mammals. Keep clear of gravel shoals and islands between 1 April and 31 July

(particularly at dawn and dusk) to minimise disturbance of breeding birds and otters. Avoid trampling and launching/landing on or near sensitive otter sites, especially in the Clifford and Whitney sectors of the river.

Some of our native species and habitats are facing a challenging future – but recreational water users including canoeists and anglers, can help protect them. There is a risk of unknowingly spreading undesirable species and disease with serious consequences. Spores and parasites can survive in damp or wet conditions for 5 to 6 days on clothing and equipment such as canoes and fishing tackle. You can help prevent harm to our wildlife by ensuring all equipment used in other freshwater bodies is thoroughly dry or disinfected with a saline solution before reusing on the River Wye.

All river users are encouraged to navigate in a way which avoids endangering or injuring other people, their boats and the bed and banks of the river. The river is there for all to enjoy so please show consideration for people, wildlife and property.

You should be aware that ignoring this advice could result in a criminal offence being committed, and you may be subject to enforcement action.

Code of conduct

The code of conduct is intended to help people enjoy the river without reducing the enjoyment of others or damaging the environment. Canoeists are asked to follow the relevant sections of the code below, which are supported by all the main user groups.

General guidance for all river users

- look after the river environment and avoid damaging banks and bankside vegetation, waterweed and gravel beds;
- avoid dragging equipment over rock slabs and boulders;
- do not disturb birds and other wildlife you find along the river. Avoid areas used by wintering wildlife, nesting birds and spawning fish in the appropriate season. Stop your activity if you are clearly disturbing wildlife;
- protect native species and habitats – use dry or disinfected equipment if used in other freshwater bodies;
- do not trespass on private banks or moorings;
- never throw rubbish into the river or leave it on the banks;
- park sensibly without causing obstruction;
- get changed out of public view;

- have special regard for beginners, as you would for learner drivers on the road;
- hail to draw a person's attention to a situation which might otherwise result in inconvenience, damage or collision. Please treat a hail as a friendly warning and not as an insult;
- please be as quiet as possible - have respect for other river users and avoid spoiling the enjoyment of others;
- be friendly and polite to local residents and try to avoid arguments;
- follow the Countryside Code and have regard for others' property.

Specific guidance for those out on the water in a boat

- all boaters must use the river in a safe fashion and have appropriate safety equipment;
- whenever possible come ashore at recognised landing places;
- do not land on gravel shoals and islands between 1 April and 31 July;
- there is an agreement for canoeing on the upper river. Details can be found at **www.wyeuskfoundation.org/navigation/index.php;**

- obey the general rules of navigation and any local byelaws;
- in particular, remember that larger boats are less manoeuvrable and cannot use such shallow waters as canoes, rafts and rowing boats;
- give way to those engaged in organised competition and have regard to any instructions given by officials;
- canoeists should take care when approaching rowing boats training in the vicinity of Hereford, Ross and Monmouth. Please comply with the Collision Regulations and stay to the right hand side of the river (when going up or downstream);
- when boating in a group try to keep together, especially when passing anglers;
- groups of young novice boaters should be led by suitably experienced responsible persons – preferably a qualified instructor;
- if in doubt about where to pass or any other query, group leaders should try to:
  - keep away from banks being fished;
  - comply with reasonable directional requests;
  - keep well clear of fishing tackle;
  - avoid loitering in pools if anyone is fishing;
  - pass anglers with as little noise and disturbance as possible.

- fishing from a boat is not allowed unless you have a valid rod licence and permission from the owner/tenant of the fishery rights. If you are boating upstream of Hay on Wye, then permission will also be required from the riparian owner.

Guidance for specific activities

The following descriptions can help identify the various types of fishing.

Coarse fishing: These anglers are often seen with an umbrella. Look out for the float 5-10m out and try to avoid their area called a 'swim'.

Fly fishing: Usually standing, wading or on bank. Avoid area opposite and, as they keep moving downstream, avoid area downstream in particular. Watch for end of line.

Game/fly fishing: Sometimes best to paddle behind them after acknowledgement.

Fishing seasons

Salmon and Sea Trout:
3 March to 17 October except above Llanwrthwl Bridge where season is 3 March to 25 October.

Non Migratory Trout:
3 March to 30 September

Coarse:
16 June to 14 March

Safety on the river

The Wye can be dangerous and has been the site of many accidents. It is at its most dangerous when there are strong currents, high water levels or cold weather conditions. Don't take risks and never underestimate the power of the river. The Wye is a fast flooding river, which can rise after heavy rain at a rate of over 30cm an hour. When in flood, it is best to keep off the river altogether.

Daily river level information

We offer an automated telephone service called River Call which provides information on levels for the River Wye. The telephone number for this service is **0906 619 7755** (BT premium rate).

Safety guidelines

Although common sense is the most important requirement, the risk of accidents can be minimised by following these simple guidelines:

- wear an approved buoyancy aid or life jacket and helmet;
- inspect rapids before 'shooting' them;
- you should never canoe alone, but if you must, let someone know where you are going, your estimated time of arrival, and let them know when you have arrived;

- make sure that you can swim at least 50 metres in the type of clothing you'll be wearing;
- carry a repair kit for your canoe, and make sure that you know how to use it;
- make sure that your canoe has built-in buoyancy or has inflated bags inside to prevent it sinking if you capsize;
- if you wear glasses, tie them with a piece of string around the back of your head in case you capsize;
- if you have not canoed before, make sure someone with experience goes with you;
- if your canoe has not been used for some time ensure that it is river-worthy.

You should learn how to cope if an accident occurs. Ideally you should be able to:

- help somebody who is in difficulty in the water or has capsized;
- give first aid;
- revive somebody who is unconscious.

Most of the above may seem obvious, but it is surprising how often they are overlooked and lead to a great deal of trouble, not only for the individual, but also for other people.

Rafting at Monmouth

Tides

Below Bigsweir Bridge the Wye is tidal and can be very dangerous, especially below Tintern. If you wish to canoe this stretch, leave Tintern no later than one hour after high water and travel down without stopping. Inexperienced canoeists are advised to avoid this stretch and should on no account travel below Chepstow, as currents in the Severn Estuary are extremely dangerous.

In an emergency phone 999 and ask for Coastguard (coastal areas) or Police (inland areas).

Finally ...
if in doubt, don't !

Health and hygiene

The quality of water in the River Wye is generally good, but unlike tap water it is untreated and contains natural bacteria and other micro-organisms. Although the risk of contracting an illness is small, there are sensible precautions which you can take to stay healthy.

Health and hygiene guidelines

- do not swallow river water;
- cover any cuts or sores with gloves or waterproof plasters;
- where possible, wash or shower after taking part in water sports, especially if you have capsized;
- wash your hands before eating;
- see your doctor if you feel ill after having taken part in water sports, particularly if you experience flu-like symptoms.

For detailed advice on the health aspects of rivers, contact your local Council's Environmental Health Officer.

Leptospirosis (Weil's Disease)

Leptospirosis is a bacterial infection caused when bacteria carried in the urine of infected animals enters the blood stream. The severity can vary from mild flu-like symptoms with severe headache, to jaundice and meningitis associated with Weil's disease.

The infection is caught by direct contact with bacteria in urine or a polluted environment. The bacteria can enter the human body through cuts, grazes, mouth or mucous membranes such as those which line the nose and ears. The usual incubation is 2 to 12 days. The illness resolves in 2-3 weeks. A few cases develop jaundice, and then the condition is known as Weil's disease.

Leptospirosis is very rare, and the deteriation into Weil's Disease even rarer. Weil's Disease is a very serious illness, and must be swiftly diagnosed and treated. The earlier leptospirosis is treated the better, so consult your doctor if you feel ill after coming into contact with water anywhere in or near the river.

Following the precautions already given will greatly minimise any possible risk.

Itinerary

We hope this guide provides useful information to help you plan and enjoy your canoeing trips.

Every effort has been made to ensure that the information is accurate. No liability can be accepted for any errors, inaccuracies or omissions. In particular, readers should note that details such as land ownership, camp sites and landing places can change from year to year.

For convenience, the river between Glasbury and Chepstow has been divided into 12 sections, each with a corresponding map. The sections are not intended as day runs and canoeists should decide for themselves how far they can travel comfortably in a day.

The first column in the itinerary is the distance from Glasbury in kilometres; the second the distance in miles and the third is the distance between points in miles.

Launching and landing

Canoeists may launch or land at the points listed without needing to get express permission, unless stated otherwise. Landing may also be made, with permission, at certain riverside campsites and through individual arrangements with some landowners.

References to right or left bank refer to the river as viewed looking downstream.

Be aware of the designated water skiing zone between Livox Quarry (ST 543979) to Chepstow Castle (ST 531946). Chepstow railway bridge to Beachley Point on the Severn is designated for all similar aquaplaning activities.

Overview of map sections

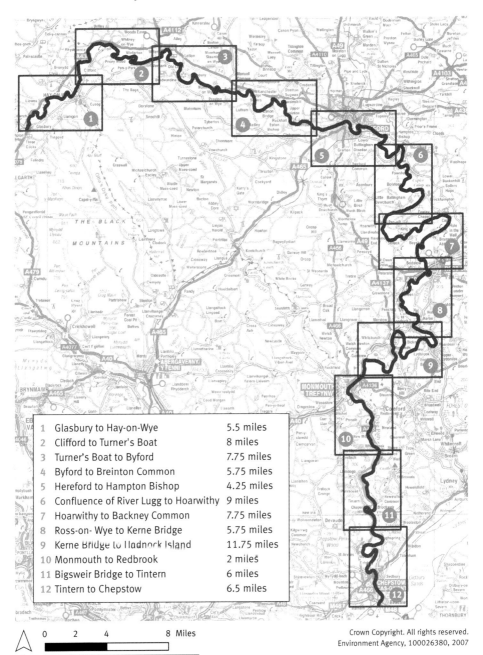

1	Glasbury to Hay-on-Wye	5.5 miles
2	Clifford to Turner's Boat	8 miles
3	Turner's Boat to Byford	7.75 miles
4	Byford to Breinton Common	5.75 miles
5	Hereford to Hampton Bishop	4.25 miles
6	Confluence of River Lugg to Hoarwithy	9 miles
7	Hoarwithy to Backney Common	7.75 miles
8	Ross-on- Wye to Kerne Bridge	5.75 miles
9	Kerne Bridge to Hadnock Island	11.75 miles
10	Monmouth to Redbrook	2 miles
11	Bigsweir Bridge to Tintern	6 miles
12	Tintern to Chepstow	6.5 miles

0   2   4   8 Miles

N

0   2   4   8   12   16 Km

Crown Copyright. All rights reserved.
Environment Agency, 100026380, 2007

Rowing at Monmouth

Map 1 Glasbury to Hay-on-Wye

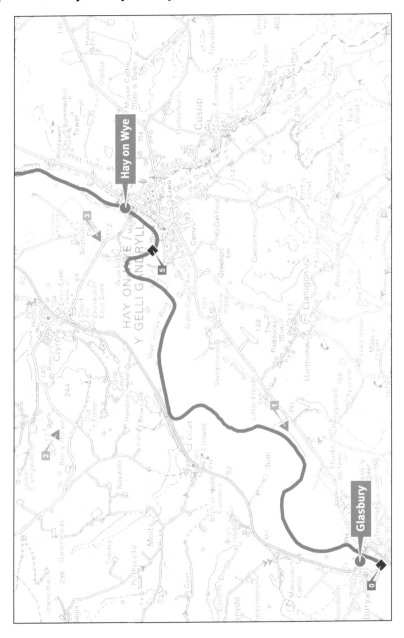

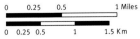

Crown Copyright. All rights reserved.
Environment Agency, 100026380, 2007

Map 1 Glasbury to Hay-on-Wye

KM	Miles	Miles		
0	0		**Glasbury (● SH PH PC CH)**	**NGR SO 179393**
			Village with post office, shops and inn. Many small rapids, usually shallow over the next few miles. These may have to be waded. Launch on the **left** bank above bridge on Glas-y-Bont Common. Canoeists are requested to launch from 18 October to 3 March between 10.00am and 4.30pm only. This is to avoid disturbing anglers – see red text below. Car park at junction of A438 and A4350.	
5	3	3	**Hollybush Inn (▲ PH CH)**	**NGR SO 198404**
8	5	2	**Boatside Weir**	**NGR SO 222427**
			Natural weir at right hand bend, normally passable **right**, but inspect at low water.	
9	5.5	0.5	**Hay-on-Wye (● ▲ SH PH PC i CH)**	**NGR SO 229426**
			Welsh border and market town with post office, stores, hotels and inns. Castle ruins, but not open to the public. For 200m below the bridge there are shallows and no clear course. Immediately below the landing place, beware of iron stakes in river bed on **right**, where Dulas Brook joins the river. These may be just below the surface. Landing on **right** bank 100m below bridge. Steps. No permission required. Small car park.	
13	8	2.5	**Clifford**	**NGR SO 242458**
			Upstream of Hay Bridge there is no established legal right of navigation. An agreement exists that facilities shared access between the anglers and paddlers. Please refer to **www.wyeuskfoundation.org** for further details.	

Upstream of Hay Bridge there is no established legal right of navigation. An agreement exists that facilities shared access between the anglers and paddlers. Please refer to www.wyeuskfoundation.org for further details.

Key to Itinerary and Maps

NGR	National Grid Reference		i	Tourist Information Centres
▲	Camp site		●	Launch/land point
PH	Public House close to river		PC	Toilet
SH	Shop		CH	Canoe hire
◆	Distance in miles from Glasbury			

Map 2 Clifford to Turner's Boat

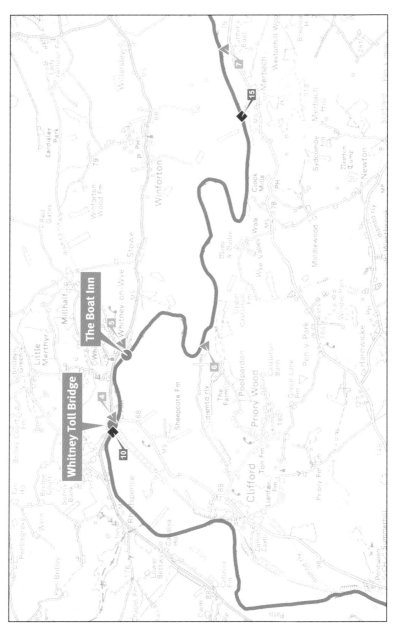

E

0   0.25   0.5   1 Miles

0   0.25   0.5   1   1.5 Km

Crown Copyright. All rights reserved.
Environment Agency, 100026380, 2007

Map 2 Clifford to Turner's Boat

KM	Miles	Miles		
13	8	2.5	**Clifford**	NGR SO 242458
			Ruins of Clifford Castle on **right** bank. Formerly an important border castle. Interesting remains of railway embankments. Do not launch/land on or near Clifford Common, sensitive wildlife site.	
14.5	9	1	**Rhydspence**	NGR SO 243473
			The border between Wales and England. The old inn on the main road (A438) **left** bank is the 'first house' in England.	
16.5	10.25	1.25	**Whitney-on-Wye (● ▲ SH)**	NGR SO 258475
			Demolished railway bridge. Beware of underwater obstructions. Closely followed by toll road bridge, built in 1774 and one of the few private bridges left in the country. Land at steps on **left** bank just upstream of bridge. Private. Fee payable for launching and use of car park. Apply to Toll Bridge Cottage (Tel. 01497 831 669). Pub and shop are in village, 10/15 minutes walk away.	
17.5	11	0.75	**Boat Inn (PH ▲ ●)**	NGR SO 269265
			There is a small rapid which sets into the left bank. From here, for four miles the river takes several large meanders and there are some shallows which may have to be waded. Land at steps on **left** bank by Boat Inn.	
19.5	12	1	**Locksters Pool (▲)**	NGR SO 269462
			Deep pool on sharp left-hand bend. Large catches of salmon have been recorded in the series of salmon pools on this stretch.	
25.5	16	4	**Turner's Boat (▲)**	NGR SO 313460

Key to Itinerary and Maps

NGR	National Grid Reference	**i**	Tourist Information Centres
▲	Camp site	●	Launch/land point
PH	Public House close to river	**PC**	Toilet
SH	Shop	**CH**	Canoe hire
◆	Distance in miles from Glasbury		

Map 3 Turner's Boat to Byford

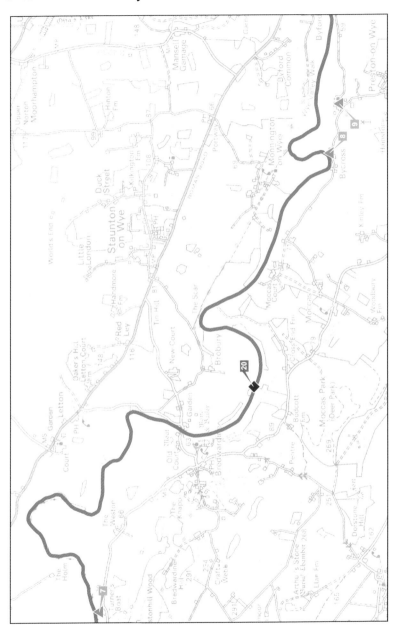

E

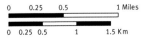

Crown Copyright. All rights reserved.
Environment Agency, 100026380, 2007

Map 3 Turner's Boat to Byford

KM	Miles	Miles		
25.5	16	4	**Turner's Boat (▲)**	**NGR SO 313460**
			The name of an island passable on the **left**. Some small rapids during the next few miles to Bredwardine Bridge.	
31.5	19.5	3.5	**Bredwardine (SH PH)**	**NGR SO 337446**
			Brick built six-arched bridge. Small village with post office, store and inn.	
34	21	1.5	**The Scar, Brobury**	**NGR SO 352445**
			High sandstone cliff on **left** bank, clothed with beeches. Look out for several large boulders in river bed, often just below the surface.	
34.5	21.25	0.25	**Moccas Court**	**NGR SO 358435**
			Large Georgian mansion on **right** bank, built in 1783. The grounds around the house were landscaped by Capability Brown.	
35	21.75	0.5	**Moccas**	**NGR SO 365433**
			Abutments only remain of Moccas Toll bridge, which stood from 1868 to 1960 when it was damaged by floods and not restored. Beware stones close to surface.	
36.5	22.5	0.75	**Bycross (▲)**	**NGR SO 376425**
37	22.75	0.25	**Monnington Falls**	**NGR SO 375429**
			See separate plan. Land on gravel bank on **left** for inspection of falls only. The channel, except in flood conditions, is to the left of the island with a small fall at the top. Inspect the whole run of fast water for obstructions and fallen trees.	
37.5	23.25	0.5	**Preston on Wye (▲)**	**NGR SO 382426**
			Church near **right** bank.	
38	23.75	0.5	**Byford (●)**	**NGR SO 400425**
			Few houses on **left** bank. Weedy shallows as far as Bridge Sollers. Landing on **left** bank 200m below pumping station, in front of black and white cottage. Overgrown area. Site of old ford. Access from road down narrow lane. No permission required. **No parking or facilities.**	

Key to Itinerary and Maps

NGR	National Grid Reference		i	Tourist Information Centres
▲	Camp site		●	Launch/land point
PH	Public House close to river		PC	Toilet
SH	Shop		CH	Canoe hire
◆	Distance in miles from Glasbury			

Monnington Falls

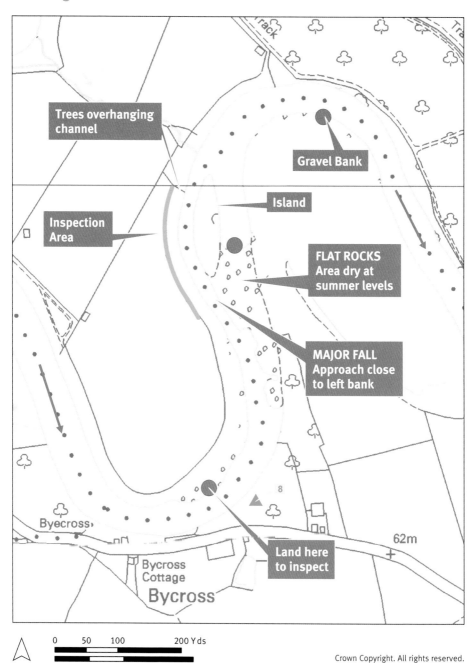

Trees overhanging channel

Gravel Bank

Island

Inspection Area

FLAT ROCKS
Area dry at summer levels

MAJOR FALL
Approach close to left bank

Byecross

Land here to inspect

Bycross Cottage

Bycross

8

62m

0   50   100   200 Yds

0   50   100   200 M

N

Crown Copyright. All rights reserved.
Environment Agency, 100026380, 2007

Monnington Falls

Land on gravel bank above falls on the **left** for inspection of falls only. You should hear the fall as you canoe round the corner. The fall and channel can be inspected as shown, by courtesy of the owner. Look carefully for the flat rocks, especially if the river has risen at all, and make sure that you can recognise the approach. Check the channel next to the island for fallen or overhanging trees. Parties should tackle the fall individually and land on the **right** bank below the island or return up the **right** hand channel to land on the flat rocks.

Map 4 Byford to Breinton Common

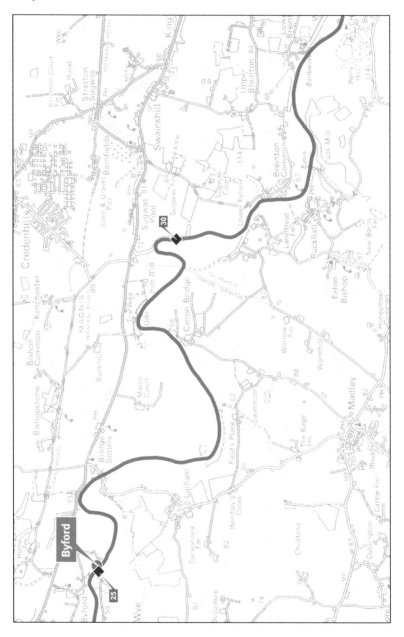

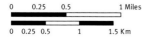

Crown Copyright. All rights reserved.
Environment Agency, 100026380, 2007

Map 4 Byford to Breinton Common

KM	Miles	Miles		
38	23.75	0.5	**Byford (●)**	**NGR SO 400425**
			Few houses on **left** bank. Weedy shallows as far as Bridge Sollers. Landing on **left** bank 200m below pumping station, in front of black and white cottage. Overgrown area. Site of old ford. Access from road down narrow lane. No permission required. **No parking or facilities.**	
40	24.75	1	**Bridge Sollers**	**NGR SO 413430**
			Bridge across river.	
43	26.75	2	**Cannon Bridge**	**NGR SO 432412**
			Few houses on **right** bank. No bridge.	
44.5	27.5	0.75	**New Weir**	**NGR SO 434419**
			No weir now. Large attractive walled garden on left, well maintained by the National Trust, with surviving masonry and a cistern from the Roman period. Gardens are open to the public from March to October.	
47.5	29.5	2	**Breinton Common**	**NGR SO 451401**
			Left hand channel round island.	
54	33.75	4.25	**Hereford (▲ ● SH PH PC i)**	**NGR SO 509396**

Key to Itinerary and Maps

NGR	National Grid Reference	i	Tourist Information Centres
▲	Camp site	●	Launch/land point
PH	Public House close to river	PC	Toilet
SH	Shop	CH	Canoe hire
◆	Distance in miles from Glasbury		

Map 5 Hereford to Hampton Bishop

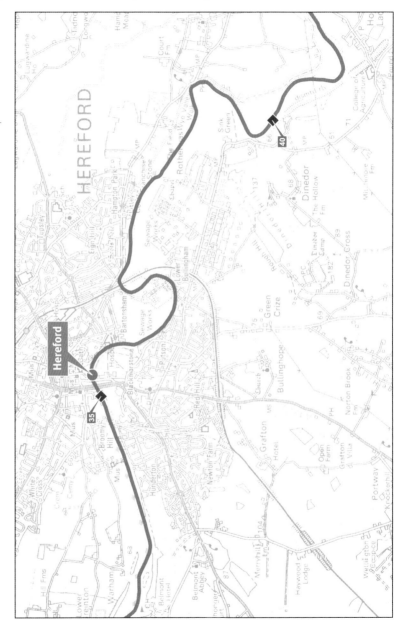

| 0 | 0.25 | 0.5 | | 1 Miles |
| 0 | 0.25 | 0.5 | 1 | 1.5 Km |

E

Crown Copyright. All rights reserved.
Environment Agency, 100026380, 2007

Map 5 Hereford to Hampton Bishop

KM	Miles	Miles		
54	33.75	4.25	**Hereford (▲ ● SH PH PC i)**	**NGR SO 509396**

Hereford grew up around an ancient river crossing, which explains its name, meaning 'ford of the army'. Among the many places of interest are the cathedral and medieval chained library, the Old House museum, Museum of Cider, city walls and the old castle site at Castle Green. A variety of river crossings include the disused iron railway bridge at Hunderton, the modern Greyfriars Bridge, the Wye Bridge built in 1490 and the elegant Victorian suspension bridge of 1898. Landing on **right** bank below old road bridge. No permission required. Car parking nearby.

KM	Miles	Miles		
56.5	35	1.25	**Bartonsham**	**NGR SO 523387**

Sewerage outfall on **left** and private road bridge, followed by railway bridge. Small rapid below railway bridge, passage to **right**.

KM	Miles	Miles		
61	38	3	**Hampton Bishop**	**NGR SO 550382**

Road (B4224) behind floodbank on **left**. The village inn, the 'Bunch of Carrots', takes its unusual name from a salmon pool nearby. No launching or landing permitted here.

KM	Miles	Miles		
67.5	42	4	**Confluence of River Lugg**	**NGR SO 565372**

Key to Itinerary and Maps

NGR	National Grid Reference	**i**	Tourist Information Centres
▲	Camp site	●	Launch/land point
PH	Public House close to river	**PC**	Toilet
SH	Shop	**CH**	Canoe hire
◆	Distance in miles from Glasbury		

Map 6 Confluence of River Lugg to Hoarwithy

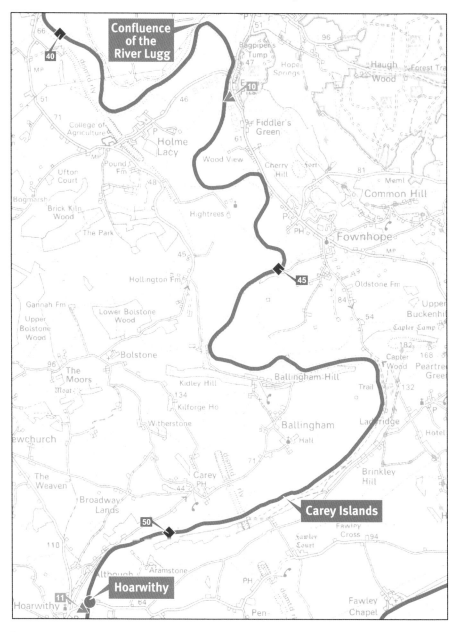

0   0.25   0.5   1 Miles

N   0   0.25 0.5   1   1.5 Km

Crown Copyright. All rights reserved.
Environment Agency, 100026380, 2007

Map 6 Confluence of River Lugg to Hoarwithy

KM	Miles	Miles		
67.5	42	4	**Confluence of River Lugg** River Lugg joins the Wye from the **left**.	**NGR SO 565372**
68	42.5	0.5	**Holme Lacy Bridge/Mordiford (▲ CH)** Modern bridge at the junction of the B4399 and the B4224. Landing at Lucksall Caravan Park downstream on **left**, but only with prior permission of owners (Tel. 01432 870 213).	**NGR SO 568364**
74	46	3.5	**Mancell's Ferry** Fishing croy on **left**. Follow signs to keep to the right around bend.	**NGR SO 575327**
75.5	47	1	**Capler Hill** Steep wooded slope on **left** bank, leading up to the double ramparts of Capler Camp, an Iron Age hill fort. A variety of birds inhabit these woods and dappled fallow deer may be sighted. From here to Ross, the river follows several large meanders.	**NGR SO 588327**
78	48.25	1.25	**Carey Islands** Group of islands with rapids in between. The best course is normally to the **right** of the first island.	**NGR SO 577307**
79	49	0.75	**Carey** Demolished railway bridge. One of three railway bridges crossing the Wye between Ross and Hereford which were dismantled when the Hereford to Gloucester line closed in 1964.	**NGR SO 570306**
82	51	2	**Hoarwithy (▲ SH ● PH)** Road bridge with village on **right** bank. Post Office, inn and the prominent 'Italianate' church of St Catherine's which has featured in at least three films. Landing on **left** bank about a quarter of a mile downstream of bridge. Prior permission should be sought from Mr Jenkins at Lower Ruxton Farm (Tel. 01432 840 223) for the **left** bank. Landing at steps on **right** bank. Fee payable for launching. Contact Mrs Roberts at Tresseck Farm (Tel. 01432 840 235).	**NGR SO 549295**

Key to Itinerary and Maps

NGR	National Grid Reference		i	Tourist Information Centres
▲	Camp site		●	Launch/land point
PH	Public House close to river		PC	Toilet
SH	Shop		CH	Canoe hire
◆	Distance in miles from Glasbury			

Map 7 Hoarwithy to Backney Common

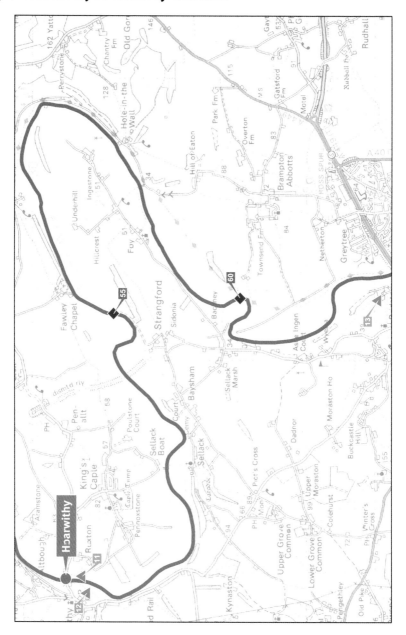

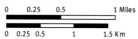

0   0.25   0.5   1 Miles

0   0.25 0.5   1   1.5 Km

Crown Copyright. All rights reserved.
Environment Agency, 100026380, 2007

Map 7 Hoarwithy to Backney Common

KM	Miles	Miles		
82	51	2	**Hoarwithy (▲ SH ● PH)**	**NGR SO 549295**
			Road bridge with village on **right** bank. Post office, inn and the prominent 'Itallanate' church of St Catherine's which has featured in at least three films. Landing on **left** bank about a quarter of a mile downstream of bridge. Prior permission should be sought from Mr Jenkins at Lower Ruxton Farm (Tel. 01432 840223) for the **right** bank. Landing at steps on right bank. Fee payable for launching. Contact Mrs Roberts at Tresseck Farm (Tel. 01432 840235).	
85.5	53	2	**Sellack**	**NGR SO 565280**
			Suspension footbridge.	
87	54	1	**Strangford**	**NGR SO 578286**
			Demolished railway bridge on the old Hereford to Gloucester line.	
88.5	55	1	**Fawley Chapel**	**NGR SO 591294**
			Interesting chapel on **left** bank (no public access from river).	
89.5	55.75	0.75	**How Caple**	**NGR SO 600298**
			The Inglestone Estate. For 2 miles downstream, the salmon pools are indicated by red and green discs fixed to the trees. Please observe these and paddle on the green side of the river.	
91.5	57	1.25	**Hole-in-the-Wall**	**NGR SO 609287**
			PGL canoe centre on left bank with private access just above rapids.	
92	57.25	0.25	**Foy**	**NGR SO 605284**
			Elegant suspension footbridge, built after an earlier structure was swept away by floods in 1919. Current restricted by small islands. Channel varies according to level. Church on right after 400m.	
94.50	58.75	1.5	**Backney Common**	**NGR SO 589269**
			A simple metal cross sits on the **left** bank. This commemorates an act of bravery by the rector of Brampton Abbotts in 1904, who died whilst saving his son and his daughter's friend from drowning. Demolished railway bridge 400m downstream at Backney. Weedy shallows.	
99.5	61.75	3	**Ross-on-Wye (● SH PH PC i ▲)**	**NGR SO 596244**

Key to Itinerary and Maps

NGR	National Grid Reference		**i**	Tourist Information Centres
▲	Camp site		●	Launch/land point
PH	Public House close to river		**PC**	Toilet
SH	Shop		**CH**	Canoe hire
◆	Distance in miles from Glasbury			

Map 8 Ross-on-Wye to Kerne Bridge

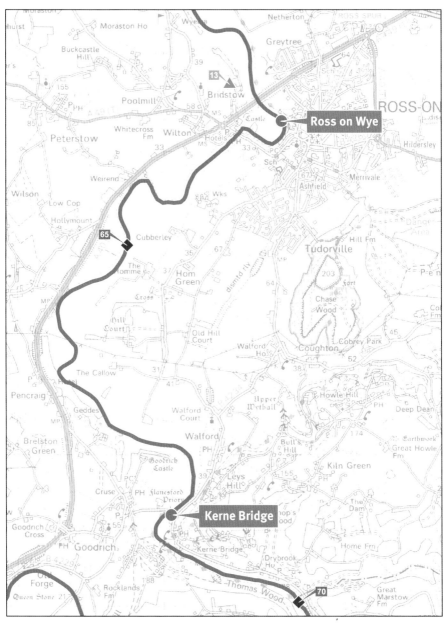

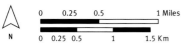

0   0.25   0.5   1 Miles

0   0.25 0.5   1   1.5 Km

N

Crown Copyright. All rights reserved.
Environment Agency, 100026380, 2007

Map 8 Ross-on-Wye to Kerne Bridge

KM	Miles	Miles		
99.5	61.75	3	**Ross-on-Wye (● SH PH PC i ▲)**	**NGR SO 596244**
			Long curve on river from motorway bridge to Wilton Bridge. The market town of Ross sits attractively on a rise above the river, with a backdrop of wooded hills. Interesting features to visit include the market house, plague cross and museums. Landing at steps on **left** bank 100m below the Hope and Anchor pub. Steps, no permission required. Car parking nearby. Please do not land or launch at Wilton Bridge.	
100	62.25	0.5	**Wilton Bridge**	**NGR SO 590242**
			13th Century castle on **right** before bridge, not open to the public. Use middle arch of the stone bridge and channel to the **right** of the island.	
107.5	66.75	4.5	**Goodrich Castle**	**NGR SO 577199**
			Impressive Norman fortification set against the skyline on the right, managed by English Heritage and open daily throughout the year.	
108.5	67.5	0.75	**Kerne Bridge (● PH PC)**	**NGR SO 581192**
			Gravel bank approximately 50m downstream of bridge. Land here to inspect the fast water for obstructions and fallen trees. Landing at steps on **left** bank 800m below road bridge. Picnic site and car park. No permission required. Goodrich village 800m to the **right**. Please do not land/launch at the bridge.	

Key to Itinerary and Maps

NGR	National Grid Reference	i	Tourist Information Centres
▲	Camp site	●	Launch/land point
PH	Public House close to river	PC	Toilet
SH	Shop	CH	Canoe hire
◆	Distance in miles from Glasbury		

Map 9 Kerne Bridge to Hadnock Island

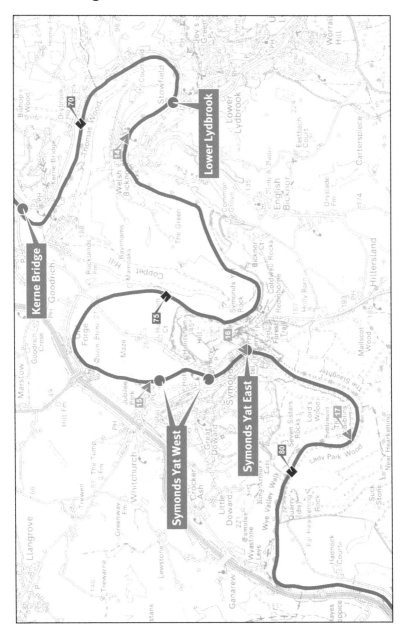

 E

0   0.25   0.5   1 Miles

0   0.25   0.5   1   1.5 Km

Crown Copyright. All rights reserved.
Environment Agency, 100026380, 2007

Map 9 Kerne Bridge to Hadnock Island

KM	Miles	Miles		
108.5	67.5	0.75	**Kerne Bridge (● PH PC)**	**NGR SO 581192**
			Gravel bank approximately 50m downstream of bridge. Land here to inspect the fast water for obstructions and fallen trees. Landing at steps on **left** bank 800m below road bridge. Picnic site and car park. No permission required. Goodrich village 800m to the **right**. Please do not land/launch at the bridge.	
112	69.5	2	**Lower Lydbrook (● PH)**	**NGR SO 596170**
			Inn on **left** bank above rapids. Keep to the **left** of the island down Lydbrook shallows. Landing on **left** bank at the steps to the picnic site and car park. Launching for individuals but NOT groups. Donations requested in honesty box.	
112.5	70	0.5	**Welsh Bicknor (▲)**	**NGR SO 591177**
			Church and youth hostel on **right** bank followed by a railway bridge, now used as a footbridge. This is an important fishing stretch. Please pass through quietly and do not linger.	
116	72	2	**Symonds Yat Rock**	**NGR SO 551172**
			Start of the long loop in river. The 150m high limestone bluff of Symonds Yat Rock is visible on the **left**.	
121.5	75.5	3.5	**Symonds Yat West (● ▲ PH)**	**NGR SO 557164**
			Landing and launching from the steps on **right** bank about 1km upstream of rapids. Car park available. Fee payable. Small passenger carrying pleasure boats based here. Landing at Ye Olde Ferrie Inne on the **right** bank. Permission required from the Inn (Tel. 01600 890 232).	
122.5	76	0.5	**Symonds Yat East (● ▲ PH CH PC)**	**NGR SO 561160**
			See separate plan. Small passenger carrying pleasure boats and a 'rope and cable' ferry for crossing the river are based here. Grade 2 rapids below the Yat can be inspected from the Peregrine Way cycle path on **left** bank. Large waves in the lower parts and congestion possible. Landing and launching from the steps on the **left** bank at the Wyedean Canoe Centre (Tel. 01600 890 129). Fee payable. Car parking available.	
124.5	77.5	1.5	**The Biblins (▲)**	**NGR SO 549145**
			Narrow suspension bridge across river. Landing for campers only.	
127.5	79.25	1.75	**Hadnock Island**	**NGR SO 538155**
			Pass either side of island. Left side usually less weedy.	
132	82	2.75	**Monmouth (● ▲ PC SH PH CH i)**	**NGR SO 512129**

Key to Itinerary and Maps

NGR	National Grid Reference	i	Tourist Information Centres
▲	Camp site	●	Launch/land point
PH	Public House close to river	PC	Toilet
SH	Shop	CH	Canoe hire
◆	Distance in miles from Glasbury		

Symonds Yat

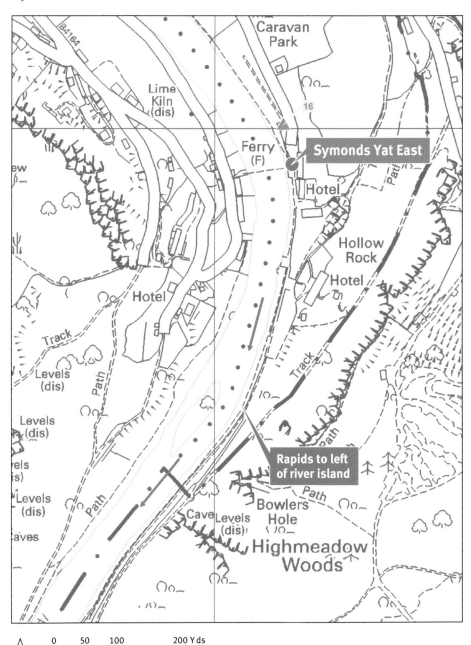

Caravan Park

Lime Kiln (dis)

16

Ferry (F)

Symonds Yat East

Hotel

Hollow Rock

Hotel

Hotel

Track

Levels (dis)

Levels (dis)

els s)

Levels (dis)

aves

Cave

Levels (dis)

Bowlers Hole

Rapids to left of river island

Highmeadow Woods

| 0 | 50 | 100 | | 200 Yds |
| 0 | 50 | 100 | | 200 M |

N

Crown Copyright. All rights reserved.
Environment Agency, 100026380, 2007

Symonds Yat

A straight fast rapid, just below the ferry, stretches the length of the island. This can be inspected from the Peregrine Way cycle path on **left** bank. Watch particularly for standing waves at the lower end of the rapid. A waymarked footpath can be followed to Yat Rock. The views are worth the climb and there is a cafe at the top.

Map 10 **Monmouth to Redbrook**

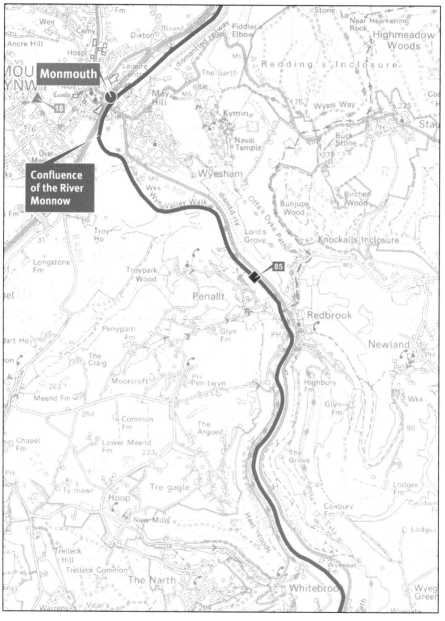

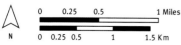

0   0.25   0.5   1 Miles

0   0.25   0.5   1   1.5 Km

Crown Copyright. All rights reserved.
Environment Agency, 100026380, 2007

Map 10 Monmouth to Redbrook

KM	Miles	Miles		
132	82	2.75	**Monmouth (● ▲ PC SH PH CH i)**	NGR SO 512129

River runs alongside main road with the attractive town to **right** with a ruined castle, market, Nelson Museum and the Naval Temple on Kymin Hill. Monmouth derives its name from the Monnow river which is bridged by a unique 14th century fortified gate house. Landing at second set of steps on **right** immediately downstream of rowing club by car park. No permission required.

132.5	82.5	0.5	**Confluence of River Monnow**	NGR SO 512122

River Monnow joins the Wye from the **right**. Beware of underwater obstructions resulting from the demolition of the two railway bridges. Rocky shallows in this area.

135	84	1.5	**Redbrook (SH PH)**	NGR SO 536100

Village with shops on **left** and inn on right. Large boulders in river above disused railway bridge now used as a footbridge. It was at Redbrook that the last recorded act of piracy took place on the River Wye when men came down from the Forest of Dean and captured two barges. There is no record of their arrest.

141	87.5	3.5	**Bigsweir Bridge**	NGR SO 539051

Key to Itinerary and Maps

NGR	National Grid Reference	i	Tourist Information Centres
▲	Camp site	●	Launch/land point
PH	Public House close to river	PC	Toilet
SH	Shop	CH	Canoe hire
◆	Distance in miles from Glasbury		

Map 11 Bigsweir Bridge to Tintern

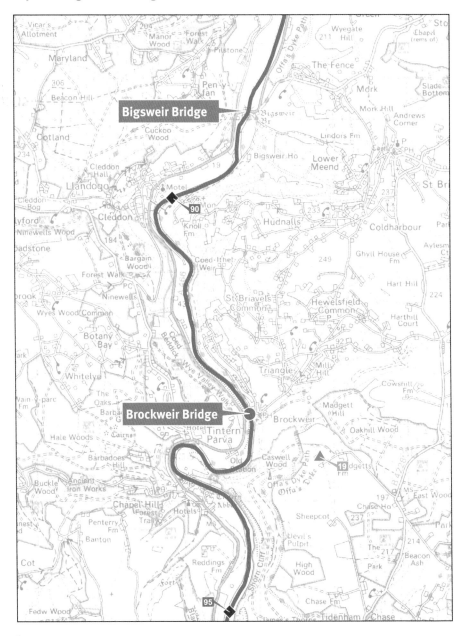

 N

0   0.25   0.5   1 Miles

0   0.25 0.5   1   1.5 Km

Crown Copyright. All rights reserved.
Environment Agency, 100026380, 2007

Map 11 Bigsweir Bridge to Tintern

KM	Miles	Miles		
141	87.5	3.5	**Bigsweir Bridge**	**NGR SO 539051**
			Narrow road bridge on the A466. Note that this is the upstream limit of tidal water. Rapids 800m downstream of bridge.	
142	88.5	1	**Llandogo (SH PH)**	**NGR SO 526041**
			Village with shops and inn on right. There are some rapids between this point and Tintern and the banks become muddy from here.	
147	91.5	3	**Brockweir Bridge (● ▲ SH PH)**	**NGR SO 539011**
			Village on left with shops and inn. Landing at restored stone landing on **left** bank just upstream of bridge, although this can be awkward and muddy at low tide. No permission required. Very limited car parking in village. Alongside the river are the remains of old quays where supplies from sailing barges were loaded and unloaded in the past. Rapids below bridge when tide is out. **Important: From this point, the river should only be used by canoeists with reasonable experience.** There is currently no landing site at Tintern or downstream after Chepstow as dangerous weirs are exposed at low water.	
149.5	93	1.5	**Old Railway Station, Tintern**	**NGR SO 536006**
			Café, Information Centre and picnic area on right.	
150.5	93.5	0.5	**Tintern (SH PC PH i)**	**NGR SO 535000**
			Village on **right** with shops and inns. Footbridge across river. Ruins of a magnificent 12th century Cistercian abbey and now popular tourist attraction on the **right**. The tide is considerable and canoeists should leave Tintern **not later than one hour after high water** and travel straight through to Chepstow. High water at Tintern is 4 hours before high water at Dover.	
161	100	6.5	**Chepstow (● ▲ SH PC i)**	**NGR SO 535944**

Key to Itinerary and Maps

NGR	National Grid Reference	i	Tourist Information Centres
▲	Camp site	●	Launch/land point
PH	Public House close to river	PC	Toilet
SH	Shop	CH	Canoe hire
◆	Distance in miles from Glasbury		

Map 12 **Chepstow**

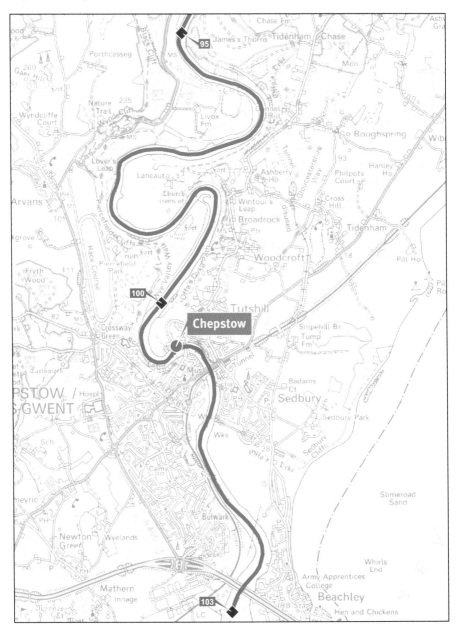

Crown Copyright. All rights reserved.
Environment Agency, 100026380, 2007

Map 12 **Tintern to Chepstow**

KM	Miles	Miles		
150.5	93.5	0.5	**Tintern (SH PC PH i)**	**NGR SO 535000**
			See map 11. Village on **right** with shops and inns. Footbridge across river. Ruins of a magnificent 12th century Cistercian abbey and now popular tourist attraction on the **right**. Important: Canoeists should leave Tintern **not later than one hour after high water** and travel straight through to Chepstow.	
161	100	6.5	**Chepstow (● SH PC i)**	**NGR SO 535944**
			Walled market town with extensive remains of a 11th century Norman castle and town gate. Landing on slipway near Boat Inn. **Please note that landing here usually involves wading through soft mud that can be very dangerous.** Limited car parking nearby.	

Canoeists are recommended **not to attempt to canoe below Chepstow** as the junction with the River Severn has very dangerous currents.

Key to Itinerary and Maps

NGR	National Grid Reference	i	Tourist Information Centres
▲	Camp site	●	Launch/land point
PH	Public House close to river	PC	Toilet
SH	Shop	CH	Canoe hire
◆	Distance in miles from Glasbury		

Accommodation

The list below is intended as a guide to camping facilities bordering the Wye. While attempts have been made to ensure that the list is as accurate as possible, it is not intended to be definitive and sites will change from year to year. You are strongly advised to check details in advance, especially for groups.

Facilities vary and some sites are no more than a farm field with a water supply. Further information about camping and other accommodation can be obtained from local Tourist Information Centres.

Key

F	field only	D	drying facilities	S	shower
Sh	shop	LP	launching/landing point	CH	canoe hire
W	water	T	toilets		

1 **Ms B Lewthwaite** Hollybush Inn Old Brecon Road Hay-on-Wye HR3 5PS T: 01497 847 371	**NGR:** River access: Open: Facilities:	**SO 198 404** On **right** bank, grounds adjoining river All year T S W D LP CH Sh B&B
2 **Mr D Lloyd Jones** Borders Hideaway Holiday Home Park Clyro Nr Hay-on-Wye HR3 5SG T: 01497 820 156	**NGR:** River Access: Open: Facilites:	**SO 197 437** No All year S W T Wb D
3 **Mr and Mrs Davies** Radnors End Campsite Radnors End Hay-on-Wye HR3 5RS T: 01497 820 780	**NGR:** River access: Open: Facilities:	**SO 225 431** No March to October T S D
4 **Mr Huxtable** Whitney Toll Bridge Whitney-on-Wye Herefordshire HR3 6EW T: 01497 831 669	**NGR:** River access: Open: Facilites:	**SO 259 475** Land at concrete steps on **left** bank - just upstream of bridge. All year T W LP

5 Mr and Mrs Taylor
The Pound
Whitney-on-Wye
Herefordshire
HR3 6EH
T: 01497 831 391

NGR
River access

Open:
Facilities:

SO 268 473
Steps on **left** bank just past
Boat Inn. Campsite across
road, opposite Inn
All year
W T LP (B&B) Sh nearby

---

6 Mrs S Mason
Oakfield Farm
Locksters Pool
Clifford
Herefordshire
HR3 5HJ
T: 01497 831 373

NGR:
River access:

Open:
Facilities:

SO 269 462
On **right** bank at left hand
bend (small shingle beach)

All year
W LP (B&B at farmhouse)

---

7 Mr D A Price
The Weston
Brewardine
Herefordshire
HR3 6DD
T: 01981 500 396

NGR:
River access:

Open:
Facilities:

SO 311 459
Shingle beach on **right**
bank, top end of
Turner's Boat
May to October
F LP

---

8 Mr and Mrs Fenn
Byecross Farm
Moccas
Herefordshire
HR2 9LJ
T: 01981 500 284

NGR:
River access:

Open:
Facilities:

SO 376 425
400 metres upstream
of Monnington Falls on
right bank
All year
T W S LP

---

9 Mr J Price
New Court Farm
Preston on Wye
Herefordshire
HR2 9JU
T: 01981 500 349

NGR:
River access:

Open:
Facilities:

SO 384 424
On **right** bank, 1km below
Monnington Falls

March to October
W LP T in summer

---

10 Mr and Mrs Williams
Lucksall Camp Site
Mordiford
Herefordshire
HR1 4LP
T: 01432 870 213
E: karen@lucksallpark.co.uk

NGR:
River access:

Open:

Facilities:

SO 567 363
On **left** bank, 200m below
Holme Lacy Bridge
1 March to 30 November
Please book for groups
of 10 or more
T W S LP Sh

---

11 Mr H Jenkins
Lower Ruxton Farm
Kings Caple
Herefordshire
HR1 4TX
T: 01432 840 223

NGR:
River access:

Open:
Facilities:

SO 549 294
On **left** bank, 400m below
Hoarwithy Bridge

Mid July to end August
F W LP

---

12 Mrs Roberts
Tresseck Farm
Hoarwithy
Herefordshire
HR2 6QJ
T: 01432 840 235
E: bookings@tresseckcampsite.co.uk

NGR:
River access:

Open:
Facilities:

SO 547 292
Steps on **right** bank

Easter to end September
F W LP T

13 Youth Hostel	NGR:	SO 591 177
Welsh Bicknor	River access:	On **right** bank above church.
Ross-on-Wye		Private landing stage
Herefordshire		marked with YHA triangle.
HR9 6JJ	Open:	March to October.
T: 01594 860300		Advance booking advised.
E: welshbicknor@yha.org.uk	Facilities:	T S W D Sh LP

14 Symonds Yat Caravan Park	NGR:	SO 556 174
Symonds Yat West	River access:	On **right** bank about 1km
Ross-on-Wye		upstream of rapids
HR9 6BZ	Open:	March to October
T: 01600 890 672	Facilities:	T W S LP CH

15 Mr and Mrs Howells	NGR:	SO 561 160
Wyedean Canoe Centre	River access:	On **left** bank above
Symonds Yat East		Saracen's Head Ferry
Ross on Wye		
HR9 6JL		
T: 01600 890 129	Open:	March to December
W: www.wyedean.co.uk	Facilities:	T W S LP CH

16 The Biblins Campsite	NGR:	SO 549 145
The Doward	River access:	On **right** bank just over
Whitchurch		1km downstream of
Ross-on-Wye		Symonds Yat rapids.
HR9 6DX		Landing for campers only.
T: 01600 890 850	Open:	March to end October
E: biblins@btconnect.com	Facilities:	T W S LP
		(organised youth groups only,
		advance booking essential)

17 Drybridge Street Caravan Park	NGR:	SO 502 129
Monmouth	River access:	No
NP25 3EX	Open:	all year
T: 01600 714 004	Facilities:	T W S

18 Dawn Cracknell	NGR:	SO 548 006
Beeches Farm	River access:	No
Tiddenham Chase		
Brockweir		
Chepstow		
NP16 7LZ	Open:	All year
T: 01291 689 257	Facilities:	T W

Please note the following corrections to the above numbering:

13 Youth Hostel	15 Symonds Yat Caravan Park
16 Mr and Mrs Howells	17 The Biblins Campsite
18 Drybridge Street Caravan Park	19 Dawn Cracknell

Also, there is no longer a number 13 campsite as shown on pages 42 & 44

Chain ferry at Symonds Yat

Tourist information centres

Chepstow:	Tel: 01291 623 722
	Email: **chepstow.tic@monmouthshire.gov.uk**
Hereford:	Tel: 01432 268 430
	Email: **tic-hereford@herefordshire.gov.uk**
Monmouth:	Tel: 01600 713 899
	Email: **monmouth.tic@monmouthshire.gov.uk**
Ross-on-Wye:	Tel: 01989 562 768
	Email: **tic-ross@herefordshire.gov.uk**
Rhayader:	Tel: 01597 810 591
	www.rhayader.co.uk
Builth Wells:	Tel: 01982 553 307
	www.builth-wells.co.uk

Useful websites

Environment Agency: **www.environment-agency.gov.uk**

Countryside Council for Wales: **www.ccw.gov.uk**

Natural England: **www.naturalengland.org.uk**

Wye Valley Area of Outstanding Natural Beauty: **www.wyevalleyaonb.co.uk**

Sport England: **www.sportengland.org**

Amateur Rowing Association: **www.ara-rowing.org**

Welsh Canoeing Association: **www.welsh-canoeing.org.uk**

British Canoe Union: **www.bcu.org.uk**

Gloucester Harbour Trustees: **www.gloucesterharbourtrustees.org.uk**

Sustrans: **www.sustrans.org.uk**

Herefordshire: **www.visitherefordshire.co.uk**

Monmouthshire: **www.visitwyevalley.com**

Forest of Dean: **www.forestofdean.gov.uk**

Wye Valley Tourism: **www.wyevalleytourism.co.uk**

Wales Tourist Board: **www.visitwales.com**

British Tourist Agency: **www.visitbritain.com**

Wye and Usk Foundation: **www.wyeuskfoundation.org**

Severn Area Rescue Association: **www.sara-rescue.org.uk**

The British Outdoor Professionals Association (BOPA): **www.the-bopa.co.uk**

The Best of Both Worlds: **www.bobw.co.uk**

Transport

National Rail enquiries
www.nationalrail.co.uk
Tel. 08457 484 950

Public Transport Information
www.traveline.org.uk
Tel: 0870 6082 608

Maps

Ordnance Survey 1:50,000 series

Sheet 161
Glasbury to 3km below Hay-on-Wye
0-11kms

Sheet 148
Hay-on-Wye to 1km above Brewardine
9-30kms

Sheet 149
1km above Brewardine to 2kms below
Hoarwithy and bend around Foy
30-84kms and 87-92kms

Sheet 162
1km below Hoarwithy to Chepstow
Excluding the bend around Foy
84-87kms and 92-161kms

**Ordnance Survey Outdoor Leisure
1:25,000 Series**

No.14
Kerne Bridge to Severn Estuary

Acknowledgements

We are indebted to **Ron** and
Ruth Shoesmith who wrote previous
editions of this guide and to the late
Allen Greenhill who was the co-author
of the first edition back in 1968 and
the inspiration behind its publication.

Wye Management Advisory Group (WyeMAG)

WyeMAG has been in existence since
1993 and has the aim of ensuring
co-operation by public bodies with an
interest in management of the River
Wye. Its membership includes:

Countryside Council for Wales;
Natural England; the Environment
Agency; Gloucestershire County
Council; Herefordshire Council;
Monmouth County Council; Powys
County Council; Sports Council for
Wales; Sport England West Midlands;
Wye Valley Area of Outstanding
Natural Beauty and representatives of
boating, fishing, conservation and
landowner interest from the users
group, the Wye Forum.

Notes